salmonpoetry

Publishing Irish & International
Poetry Since 1981

The Road, Slowly is the ground-breaking debut collection of love poems from award-winning Irish poet, Liz Quirke. With an assured voice, her poems weave through the experience of becoming a wife and mother in a collection of considerable lyrical beauty. Her poetry ploughs new thematic ground with confidence and subtle, delicate observations. Same-sex parenting in modern Ireland; non-biological motherhood and ways in which the past can inform the present are explored with courage. Quirke celebrates the connection between parents and children within a non-nuclear family with scalpel sharpness and a discerning eye. Her poems pay tribute to the achievement of family.

the arts council
chomhairle
ealaíon

funding
literature
artscouncil.ie

The Road, Slowly

Liz Quirke

Published in 2018 by
Salmon Poetry
Cliffs of Moher, County Clare, Ireland
Website: www.salmonpoetry.com
Email: info@salmonpoetry.com

ISBN 978-1-912561-12-4

COVER ARTWORK: *The Road, Slowly* by Yvonne Hennessy –
www.yvonnehennessy.com
AUTHOR PHOTOGRAPH: Yvonne Hennessy
COVER DESIGN & TYPESETTING: *Siobhán Hutson*

Printed in Ireland by Sprint Print

*Salmon Poetry gratefully acknowledges the support of
The Arts Council / An Chomhairle Ealaíon*

for Yvonne, Juno and Nova, my loves

Acknowledgements

Acknowledgements are due to the editors of the following publications in which some of these poems first appeared: *An Áit Eile*; *Boyne Berries*; *Crannóg*; *Hennessy New Irish Writing* (The Irish Times); *Inkroci* (trans. Italian); *Impossible Archetype*; *Irish Examiner*; *Listowel Writers' Week Winners' Anthology 2017*; *One* (Jacar Press, US); *Poethead − An Index of Women Poets*; *Poetry Day Mixed Tape 2017* (Lagan Online); *Skylight 47*; *Southword*; *Spontaneity*; *The Bogman's Cannon*; *The Best New British and Irish Poets 2016* (Eyewear Publishing, UK); *The Hidden and the Devine: Female Voices in Ireland* (A New Ulster); *The Ofi Press* (Mexico); *The Stony Thursday Book*.

"Juno" and "Nurture" were nominated for the 45th Hennessy New Irish Writing Emerging Poetry Award and shortlisted for the 2015 Cúirt New Writing Prize. "Sculpture" won the 2015 Poems for Patience Competition. "The Trees and The Breeze" won the 2017 Listowel Writers' Week Originals Short Poem Prize. "Daedalus Speaks to Icarus, His Son" was longlisted for the 2016 Dermot Healy Poetry Award. "Rite" was shortlisted in the Over The Edge New Writer Of The Year 2012 competition. In 2017 as part of a collaboration between Liz Quirke and Yvonne Hennessy, "Nurture" was reimagined in an audio-visual installation titled "The Weight of Chaos" which was shown at CCAM in Galway and Surface Tension: the Members' Exhibition at Interface Residency, Inagh Valley during Clifden Arts Festival and in Detroit Stockholm, Sweden.

I would like to express my gratitude to the following individuals and organisations for their support over the years: Máire Holmes and the Writers in Res, Eleanor Hooker, Martina Evans, Leanne O'Sullivan, Elaine Feeney, Aoibheann McCann at Utter Word, Ruth McKee, Kevin Higgins & Susan Millar DuMars at Over The Edge, Felicia McCarthy, Rob Childers, Lorna Shaughnessy, Rebecca Anne Barr, the Skylight Poets, The Poetry Bus, Doneraile Literary and Arts Festival, Bray Literary Festival, Dani Gill, The Galway Review, Cúirt International Festival of Literature, Margaret Flannery and Galway University Hospitals Arts Trust, James Harrold, Alannah Robins at Interface Inagh, Siobhán Hutson and Jessie Lendennie at Salmon Poetry, Meadhbh Ní Eadhra, Leeann Gallagher, Allison Long, Clodagh Murray, Fiona Deane for the use of her kitchen table where this manuscript really began to take shape. My thanks to the Quirke family, especially my parents, Maureen and Tom, for giving me the words and the Hennessy-Quirke family for giving me the inspiration. This collection would never have been possible without the support and love of my wife, Yvonne Hennessy. Finally, I would like to thank my daughters, Juno and Nova, for teaching me that the road is at its best when travelled slowly.

Contents

Chapter 3 - Water I Scoop with Netted Fingers

Epilogue

Prologue

I Don't Write You Love Poems Anymore

All my words are kept for the children,
sequestered to chronicle little tempests and successes,
swaddles of coats and jumpers, boots slightly large
on feet as the oldest takes her chances
in every puddle she can find.

Instead of the resting hollow of your hip,
my words now know the fit of skull and cheek
against my shoulder, the weight
of each of our babies as they fall asleep.
I write the rasp of breaths lovely in my ear,
how pillows furrow with their heavy heads.

I compress this life into a collage
of simile and verse. Discover
that writing them is like carrying a lake
in my hands, too much lost
by the time pen meets page.

In our years together, love, I have written you
with all the heart a pen can hold, your warmth
recalled in every city we passed through.
Nights wrapped in hotel sheets
after hours drinking with strangers,
the heady risks of our early years.

These days those stories don't fall easy into ink.
My poems exist in how small faces startle
when the light switch alters evening in the kitchen,
the way little fingertips pad a pane of glass
in the burnt umber twilight before the rain comes.

Boluisce

I root my fingers, burying them back and down;
a twist into black acidic soil,
deeper than anything man-made.

I push to the graves of the lake families;
generations who lived and died by the water.

I pay my respects the only way I know,
by kneeling in the sodden earth
and sinking parts of me towards parts of them.

I do what no record does and remember their passing,
their assimilation back to the land.

I want them to teach me how to inhabit this place,
to reanimate and diffuse their knowledge into my urban bones,
our times merging under a canopy of living skin.

Chapter 1

More than Bone and Flesh

Housework

i

Slamming around in the kitchen,
your mother prepares the space for you,
ties rhythm to her movements

like a knot in loose apron strings.
Countertop cleared, plates stacked clean, concealed
behind cupboard doors, as if order in the mundane

will tick some unknown box and draw you in.
Taps scald. Her skin pinks as though slapped
by the lack, all our empty hours,

the flutter of another calendar leaf as the months turn,
the absence of kiddie cutlery, sippy cups on the draining board.

ii

Those long months we searched for a home,
any assembly of someone else's memories,
a vessel to hold our not-yet family.

Worse in the mangle of my recollection,
that rambling shell we nearly bought,
all romance, ivy spidered through walls,

character we couldn't take on.
We've talked ourselves back up those stairs
once or twice, to the landing's turn,

each time deciding silently the bedrooms needed
too much work, our plans couldn't wait.

Waiting Room

There is a room wide as a football pitch
and narrow as a cupboard.

Off to one side, a low table bears lever arch folders
a person can thumb through, photographs of babies,
little navy jumpers, twins in pink onesies,
with some teeth and no teeth,
with newborn down on tops of heads or first wisps.

There is a waiting room wide as a football pitch,
narrow as a cupboard, where people sit quietly,

clutch soft plastic cups of ice cold water,
where chairs are a decent size and spaced
so couples don't have to touch each other
unless they want to.

There is a waiting room with a projector screen
at one end, large as a feature window, explaining

through vibrant graphics to the people sitting quietly,
people who have more than likely researched
the building and its occupants
to floorboard detail, what will happen
in treatment rooms they haven't seen yet.

There is a room, where people sit quietly, wait
in twos or ones as though all conversation led them there

but finished earlier in the carpark, or exhausted itself
the evening before over pots of tea, when talk pushed
into the night about cycles, hormones, injections,
whispers of what they would bargain to know
the feeling of their baby's foot between their fingers.

There is a waiting room, silent
but for shoes shuffling on matte carpet, quiet

but for the hum of the water cooler,
the crisp diction of the volume controlled radio,
pop-songs by girls promising
something new, crooning with sentiment
about an abstract forever, never to know
how their voice hangs over people who can only wait

for their names to be called
by the woman in scrubs with the clipboard.

What Has My Body Done

Even though the tree shares bark and branch,
the sky was promised leaves.

Even though the lake can't count itself in fish,
it mutely panics into a river.

Have you ever watched a magpie
gut a field mouse?

Witnessed it slink threat-like from rushes
with a small body pierced in its thick black beak,

all brightness pulled out, picked over
like the ransacked contents of a jewellery box,

sifted until the thief can raise its head, satisfied
with a mouth full of still-warm heart.

Carving

With talon hands
I write your name across the sky,
pluck threads from cloud formations
to weave letters.
A composite of wild precipitation
and weather-weak remains,
I hold you suspended,
an ink blot, a Rorschach test.
Curlicues and spirals that fall to wax,
hardening when gravity fails.
This is our embarrassment.
Our failure to coalesce.
When skin splits and blood runs
and the life we planned vanishes into dust.

Lucky

Under a shaded frame with places set to celebrate,
a woman angles and without removing her spoon
from the potato salad, sears the child at her shoulder,
"I wish you had never been born."

The girl, no more than eight, swallows her dismissal,
washes it down with a mouthful of burning summer,
her flushed cheeks inverting their heat to cleanse her palate.

Her mother, mouth now full, eagles
the assembly, lands carrion eyes on us.
"You're lucky, girls. They're horrible little things.
Never have children."

We sit side by side, you and I, thigh nearly touching thigh
as in the rooms we have spent our time, waiting
to be led from grey carpet to grey walls,
from the tick of one timepiece to another, seasons
of hours and minutes, cycles with a before and after.

We sit in plastic chairs, the same posture
as when we have depersonalised the personal
into dark ink and the smallest tickable boxes.

This woman waits now, consumes the stiff line of your neck.
No words left to say under this gazebo,
no action but to pluck the spoon from her slackened grip
and deliver her the image of her own distortion.

Your cutlery clicks together on the plastic table.
We will leave soon. Your appetite is gone.
The unlucky months have killed your taste buds,
swathed our journeys home in silence.

Newborn

You will come to me, perfect,
skin alabaster, a primed canvas,
a space for ink and paint,
light and shade in a fleshy bundle.

Scared and hopeful, I know
I will leave fingerprints,
watermarks on your surface,
reduce your glass to less than perfect.

My eager breath will frost failures
onto places they have no business.
Without intention I will change you.
My doubts will mar the pristine.

As our years together thin away,
skin will peel, little by little.
A layer from me, a layer from you.
Words between us will catch, leaving us ragged.

As much as I may fail without meaning
and mourn every sliver of destruction,
I promise to be with you, a constant,
naive and imperfect.

Fall At 33 Weeks

She said it was like falling
on a small dog,

that she felt each rattling jolt
of baby bones

barely wrapped in paper thin skin
push down to meet concrete.

She said she heard her own weight
cover and crunch that small shape,

all four pounds.

She didn't have time to catch herself or react,
didn't know what had happened

until strangers
lifted her from the steps.

She surrendered to the slope of a hospital bed,
her body to ill-angled foam,

lay prone as machines read the signs we couldn't see,
traced brain waves and pulses to tell us the worst.

The Painting

Standing in your pelt in the living room,
had you ever been more yourself?
You had called in the painter
to put a frame on narrowing days,
recalled a dream of yours, from before
you were meant to dream such things,
that if your body ever became more than bone
and flesh, you would surrender to your skin,
commit it all to canvas.

A Friday after work, beyond the due date
and you well ready to meet the person
who loomed within you, to know
her toes, her heels, her elbows
from more than car-ride Eagles singalongs
and maternity shop browsing.

That Friday you were set
when the artist came to make new
our domestic space
with gradients of tone and shadow,
boards shifting minutely under his feet
as our furniture became other than shapes we knew,
the room different than we lived in it,
sheets layered to squeeze the light out,
draping lines that made no sense
till you stood within them.

For the swell of an hour,
lit from the floor, you held yourself
and her too, leaning this way and that,
front foot and back and in repose,
so he could conceive your view from every angle,
choose how to isolate your forms
and pull you both from a blackened canvas,
lull the two of you into the corner of this very room
where you hang always in the before time.

Nurture

In the nine months I didn't nourish you,
I made notes, I studied the seasons
for ingredients to encourage your growth.
Scraps of paper, post-its hidden
in case anyone would view my thoughts,
pity my trivia of leaves and berries.

A mom yet not a mother,
a woman yet not a woman.
My preparation took place in private,
not in maternity wards or hospital corridors,
but in the hallways of my mind
where I could put up pictures, timelines,
fill cork boards with plans.

As the folic acid built your brain stem
I collated ideas to stimulate it further,
mapped journeys for us,
paths we could walk together,
a staggered relay to start
when your other mother
passed your tiny form to me.

And I could see myself holding your hand,
using my limbs to scaffold the structure
your mother put so beautifully in place.
I am your mom without the biology of mothering.
All I have for you is my heart, my brain, my lists of things,
all but those nine months when I was waiting.

Vacancy

I have this time when she is asleep
to scrawl my thoughts.
She is lodged into my shape,
a comfort from thigh to chest.

Before her, I believed
I claimed the space I was meant to.
When I relaxed I assumed
my hollows held their own.
But there must have been a lack,
a vacancy that called to her,

because she arrived and fitted into place
into the arc of my body on this bed,
into parts of my days
I didn't know were empty.

Juno

I gave you a warrior name.
Brazen, audacious,
a statement of intent.

After the third scan,
I set out across the world's mythologies
to uncover the name to herald you.

I found you in the pages
of an old hardback,
barely two inches in a row of columns.

Sensible, poised,
waiting for me to arrive and collect you
at the obvious conclusion,
assured that this is where you had always been.

For weeks after our first meeting
you kept me company.

Your name fell in ink from my pen
until that sturdy bulk of letters
came as familiar as my own.

The shape of you rolled around my mouth
like a boiled sweet,
pushing taste to unreachable corners,
forcing my buds awake until I had a full sense of you.

Your vowels whispered through my lips,
soft as the steam after a kettle click.

And when you arrived, emergent, slow to pink,
but quickly, so quickly,
your name gushed out of my mouth
like your first breath,

triumphant,
your first victory,
your battle cry.

Nocturne With Bathtime

Cradling your neck in the cup of my fingers,
soft your putty skull, thin in my hand.

Sturdy now, a more conscious mass,
your breaths call time to our steps.
Movement cued with your first cry,
slipping your arms through your vest the first time.
Around you we pad easy,
pass you off to each other, steady hands.

Cradling your neck in the cup of my fingers,
soft your putty skull, thin in my hand.

This rhythm makes all sense,
ingrained in our limbs with your arrival.
Mothering you is a sweeping affair.
It is powder light with a hint of chamomile,
a dip to warm water, swing to clean towels,
swooping to finish with a burnishing forehead kiss.

Night Vision

Between our tired forms, you stay alert,
eyes wide as our bed
becomes your playground.

Claiming a strip of sheet and quilt
where your small body can collapse,
jump up and collapse.

Your arms stretch out in a backwards flop
and you relax supine until sleep comes.

You enjoy these ill-disciplined nights,
free from the confines of your cot,
when teething or some other fever
keeps you close.

Jittering with extra energy, so confident
we can contain your movements,
trusting that our shapes will hem you in

when you fall, that our arms will tether you to our earth.

In The Dead Of

At that time of night,
hours when air only clots,
feels jelly thick
around limbs
too numb to stand.
Knuckles soft
with sleep,
ankles weak
as though boiled.
Your cries meld
into the walls.
The sounds
from your mouth
move in sinking waves.

The Shining Swell

While the night burns,
you work the fortune of a tooth from embers.
Awake since you closed your eyes,
only small-hour whispers nurse the sting.

Growth hurts. It's in the shining swell beyond
your lips where words have yet to bud.

In the garden, rushes buckle
under the lake's furrowed bluster.

While sweat beads at your temple,
all I can tell you, daughter,
is that the storm has to dampen sometime,
this haunting will fade in the wilt of memory.

Teeth

Your new teeth allow you to howl
like the quietest of wolves.

Small opinions rattle as bone appears
from under its tether of gum,

putty-soft enamel,
enough to split a sin of strawberries.

Your mouth renders you older,
mature in your twenty-one week skin.

Pliable cheeks, ruddy topography
of your dimpled chin,

where reddened dribble runs in rivulets,
berry seeds in the corners of your lips,

semi-colons to your smile.

As you gain traction in the world,
more sure of your place in it,

your voice bears a weight,
chimes in with warbling pitch.

Working your fruit, you double-task
by tracking us around the kitchen.

Not sure how to call us to heel,
you echo a return command,

nothing more than the clicking
and sucking of skin against muscle,

but we hear you all the same,
a humming in the blood,

freckling phrases into our skin like braille.

Sculpture

With a teaspoon, I sculpt fruit to fit
your tiny palm, hourglass is best.

The shape gives you a place to clamp your fingers.
Knuckles pucker with the work of it.

If you are lucky, by the time it reaches your mouth,
there is still juice left, eating and drinking in one.

Often though, it decorates your sleeve which you wave
like a soggy flag, happy gumming through the meat of it.

I approach each ripened apple the same way
as a woodturner his lathe.

With my kitchen chisels, I reveal worlds inside skin,
bring you through bark to places you can't yet go on your own.

I show you each careful movement, the pierce of my blunt knife,
the twist of wrist and hand, counter clockwise, an easy stroke,

predicting that somewhere down the line our places will change
and with my instructions in the back of your mind,

you will face your own child,
with your own fruit and show them new worlds.

CHAPTER 2

All the Hidden Truths

Sentinel

Sure-footed and still
under leaves as drops fall
from above you.
Steady stare into the half-light,
listening with winter's ear
to the buckle and crush
of frost under cattle feet.
Shot and sulphur
will not shift your purpose
as you survey all around,
waiting for the cracks to appear.

Counterfeit

Easy as talk at a child's party, I cluster as one of their number.
When the men fade, attention turns from woman to woman,
   lap to lap.

I do not surrender my baby to the communal hold.
"Are you tired? Is she three months?"

How these words shape me. They set me up in a hospital bed,
girded, pressing, sweat and spit when the contractions build,

tears when the work of my body is over.
Two small questions assume the set of my womb,

the establishment of milk, a healthy supply
given the child who gums into the fabric covering my shoulder.

Propriety requires my answer to be my lack
of sleep, chapped nipples, swollen ducts,

all the bruisings and restitchings of childbirth. I hum and rock the baby,
knowing the moment my interlocutor sees through me.

The line of her lips tells that she knows the lie of my body,
sees camouflage in the extra weight at my hips, subterfuge

in the curve and sag of my breasts. It is her final sweep that does it,
her crosscheck of features, my face against the smaller one.

I see her check my measurements, the distance
from eyes to ears, lips to chin, the cleft I do not have.

I see her hold these facts loose as coins in her palm,
I see her put those parts of me between her teeth

and clamp down, finding nothing but a lightweight metal,
a hollow ring, a counterfeit.

Reflection

I run water till the tiles sweat.
My skin owes me this discomfort.
Every pore should barely cope.

Public and private scattered my insides today,
smeared lines like fresh paint after fingernails.

I am dropped coins picked over,
smallest values raked to a gutter.

I've been discarded like cracked delph
and I cannot shake the handling.

I had to come in here, snap the cord
to blaze the telling glass,
ease eyes over my body in that way of strangers,
how their hungry mouths linger wet
around words like "*real*", words like "*mother*",
dart-like demands for clarity.

Tonight I try see it for myself,
assess each part until all I know are differences.

I stand unadorned,
hold my body's gaze until it's all there,
the telltale lack of marks,
softness that proves all I didn't do.

I look till I can hardly stand it.
This two-foot by three-foot glass holds it all,
a telling stare I cannot break.
Can't look away, I can't avoid this body
that did nothing to make her.

Auto-Immune

Who knew a body could hate,
hurt itself like a teenage girl with a razor blade
pulled from safety casing,
or, if she's feeling particularly disenfranchised,
a hammer firm to the soles of her feet,

maybe heavy boots slammed
by her own hand across her toes.
There isn't a single word for the way bone
and sinew tighten from the inside,

no name for the weakness
that lives in the heart of pain.

Is there a medical term for walking
on cobblestones without stopping?
Counting 1 to 100 over and over,
a metronome set to the pace of passers-by.

Will the consultant's lexicon stretch
to colour the grimace kept from a face,
the inside-cheek bite hidden,
admit to the knowledge that the body
is more cunning this time?

Ri, Ro, Rem

i

With that known scent of chemicals hypoallergenic,
the nurse works over the hand far more year-worn than her own,
sweeps cooling wetness from heel to fingerwell and back again,
tender as charity.

The older hand, cannula in and stiffly set, leans into this kindness,
skin cardboard from lack of movement,
knuckles, creases and nail beds
accept the unrequested comfort, for the little time it lasts.

Hidden in the corner of this scrubbed space,
conversation as effortless as buttering bread rumbles,
listing names, places, where to get the good potatoes.

ii

As the nurse drips me up,
all needles and clear tubing,
panic wrenches across your face.
It's in the widening of your daybreak eyes,
the colouring stretch of your features.

We had the kitchen part of the morning together,
hot, buttered toast after eye-blink showers,
the girls dressed in bright pastels and out.

On the Coast Road, you talked
me through the colours of the Burren,
rendered Galway Bay through prisms of light,
ebbing greens and blues.

The plan had been a pre-anniversary brunch,
but all I offered was black coffee,
in a blank cardboard cup, communal milk,
a single brown sugar in the hospital canteen.

I wanted you stationed across from me
for a stolen while,
knowing that our eventual place
would be side by side
on the leather waiting room couch,

jitters threading our fingers together,
palms flat, except for the bowed concave
where unuttered words are stored.

iii

Two floors above Poets' Corner,
in a chair that my private purse is paying for, I sit.

The day moves in stages: conversation initiated
so consent is gently gathered; three tablets,

a pouch of steroids while bones settle
into a medically calculated recline; finally, the poison.

The hanging bag, heavy as autumn fruit that no-one picked,
casts its shadow from the space above my head.

I hear the roll call of names so familiar now: *Rituximab* (me),
Roactemra (old lady across the way), *Remicade* (next door)

Words possessing the oldest syllables, ones a teething baby
uses for comfort against cold pears. Ri, Ro, Rem,

part of my mouth has worked around these words before.
I unpick the phonemes, wonder why the tools of healing
    sound so hopeless.

In the private hospital, three floors above
the external water feature and Alice in Wonderland chess board

I learn, at thirty one, what it takes a body like mine to survive
but not what breaks it.

Poison

Up and out it comes like his last breath,
the worst one, rattling guttural of an emptying throat,
the whisper of used-up lungs.

The night he leaves, you channel the poison that finished him;
easy as milk – questions of untended graves,
forgotten family – churned within your small body.

There is method to this night-time vigil,
our hushed steps as we watch your fever break, unaware
that tonight, he is the only one afforded any sleep.

Rite

There will be a changing of the guard,
if such ceremony will be allowed,
a dusting down of dampers
to purge all lamps and lights.
Shops will mourn from their facades,
black-ribboned in the old way.
Passers-by will nod and scuttle
to spurn the mists of death.
Great coats will be sponged as they were before,
and shoes spit-shone to a pitch-like gleam.
The footfall slap will ring out around the streets.
Wedding services kept for cakes
and sour-crust dry triangles
will peek under from muslin fabric,
while whiskey flows like speech.
Clocks will chime only grief notes,
humming deep into the silence.
Eyelid mirrors will reflect the dark beneath.
Running along on idle tracks,
children will be shunned
from the adult world,
palming flowers in the breeze
to mimic final kisses not received.

Daedalus Speaks To Icarus, His Son

How it is that I who can coax stone
into labyrinthine detail could fail
to build the basics of your senses?

My greatest success stands as a reliquary
to forever keep what little was gathered of you,
your robe, splinters of your bones,

slivers of pride among scattered,
waxless feathers, fingertips still reaching
towards the sky.

My son, you surrendered to the vanity
of a daring death, tested yourself
in elemental ways you were not born to conquer.

No Apollo you, what was your last thought?
Did you call Father into the wind as you fell?
Or did arrogance that the next upward gust was yours

keep you silent as the water rushed to fill your mouth?
The women say their mothering ears still hear your cries,
their night-feed hearts slowed to a dimming thrum

when you failed to breach the surface.
They detailed in that way of women
how it feels to see a child's body broken,

because you were a child to them,
and they can cry for you and remember
your newborn skull warm in the palm of their hand.

Salvage

New rooms I will build from you, bones and all.
The laboured rungs of your spine will stack neatly,
beautiful furniture. Angled strength
siphoned through your forearms,
trust wrought from the ballast lines of your limbs.

I will unpack my flimsy particles for assessment.
If you see fit, spread me out, inventory what remains,
assemble my unruined elements,
joints, anything you can salvage.
Wrap tight, firm till I set and can stand alone.

These rooms will be a composite of us both.
You, the shape, register of craft.
My fingertips will press your intercostal
muscles to cornice definition,
push your art to show itself.

Debris thickens your knuckle bends
and fist-curled territories,
but this is our arrangement,
where my tiles slot into our mosaic
and you are the setting clay that holds.

Once done with your reclamation,
survey the scree, hold the smallest parts together,
dust my skin with cement-rough hands.
Through the heat of your palms
I will come back,

resembling what I was before,
but better because of you.

Women Poets Teach Me How To Be A Woman

i

First I was shown a world through a window,
invited to witness at seventeen
how one woman's heat could be passed
to another, the comfort and risk
of a closed door, delicate and sweet
as a promise. The way soft lighting
can bruise silence into a throat;
signposts in *The Yellow Room*
all pointing to images in my own mirror.
Stanzas thick with language I ached
to translate and when I finally found the words,
tasted them in the curve of a pale neck,
I spoke them aloud, not in my voice but hers,
recognised the *rabbit's foot* dim with dust,
cooling jewels alone in their beds and
all night I felt their absence and I burned.

ii

Years later love led me to where women
waited with children young like mine,
their lexicon full of all I couldn't name,
handed over heavy as bad news.
Details penned precisely, I read
till I understood the burning in my gut.
The loss they knew, those women
who *loved with an almost fearful love.*
They filled their books with ways my own parents
remembered their small son, gone too soon from them.
These women put into words
what a swing looks like when a child
no longer plays in it, how bags of clothes
drag in a tearful *hoisting to an attic's dark.*
One assured that *the art of losing isn't hard to master,*
but how wrong she turned out to be, how wrong.

Four Parts Distinct

Birds warble backwards, flowers retract to buds.
Four parts distinct, our rounded edges
should sweeten with the lock of a well-worn joint,
the slide of wood on wood, lattice strong.

The blueprint makes clear where we need
to place ourselves, lever and counter lever,
but today we witness the whole thing fall to bits —
cups throw off their handles, decide to be bowls,
forks melt down their tines, reinvent themselves as knives.
We linger in the discomfort of a shoe unhappy to be merely a shoe.

The days we don't fit, the sky doesn't warm anything,
just shows up the streaks on our windows
from the last storm, the fug of a heavy gutter.

We four talk at the same time. Try find a roof in the garden,
language without language. No one is hungry at the same time.
We best take a saw to the table, deal it out in limbs,
take mine to the fire that won't light.
No one is tired at the same time.
A black horizon is nothing but a cave to shout into.
Whose voice is this?

The days I have too many legs and not enough arms,
I wish a bigger footprint for the house
so I would have the choice of hiding places.

Until you come and tell me we are better than this.
        And I listen.

Until you come and tell me we are better than this.
        And I hear you.

Until you make me go outside and walk the boundary
of our life.
        And I do.

Reassemble myself at each fence post,
until I see the house we own together from every angle,
pet the dog, quiet down just long enough
to see us four, separate and distinct,
holding to the slope of a home
we salvaged for ourselves.

Where All The Light Can Gather

i

Words that sound like the minor
chords of a mandolin
float upwards as we drink
cheap wine on someone else's dollar.
Sloshed into foggy tumblers,
corked and soupy.
You said you would bring me
to Meeting House Square
for oysters at the market,
but instead we sit here,
your feet nearly touching mine.

ii

I carry a hint of you, always.
Small coded shapes
to project your form
and conjure your silhouette
where all the light can gather.
Words skew the senses,
score the edges of perception.
When we are separate,
the space beside me thickens,
my cheek wears your invisible kiss,
my arm the warm ghost of your hand,
the print of clasped fingers.

Romance

Drunk on each other, we savour our one-star hotel room
with the twin wooden-frame beds, the Chubb key in the lock,
the type I imagine Dev pressed into a candle.

Drunk later again in a Venetian hole-in-the-wall bar,
you defy gravity and the saturation of your molecules,
balance one foot on the toilet cistern, the other against the wall,

brace yourself on the dry block,
rise to scrawl our names, the date,
a monument to our Ryanair sale seats,

and with a pencil made blunt by beer-mat sketches
drawn on demand for honeymooners,
you write us as stars into a pale constellation, immortalise us

in the firmament of this student-quarter bathroom,
letter our young love in plain sight
on the most unlikely canvas ever to bear your mark.

Portraits Of My Lover

After Selima Hill

Portrait Of My Lover As A Floorboard

You prefer the intimacy of bare feet,
skin pressing on knots,
pores speaking to the tree you once were,
the one you dream of becoming again.

Portrait Of My Lover As A Cup Of Tea

You eye me from the mantelpiece,
remind my hands that they work best
when wrapped around you,
a comfort best consumed immediately.

Portrait Of My Lover As A Nightdress

Hushed cotton, sleep trembles
in the crosshatch of your threads,
blinking like sound until you close
yourself around me button by button.

CHAPTER 3

Water I Scoop
with Netted Fingers

Nova

i

You exist for now only
in the abstract, the space
between fingers
when hands reach.

You live in the instant
before words are spoken,
when breaths hold
and a tongue moves
to press against the promise
of a first syllable.

You exist for now only
to our knowledge,
too early to alert the masses,
our happy contraband,
our welcome stowaway.

We have weeks yet to keep you
to ourselves and this quiet
secrecy is more real to us
than abstract generally allows.

ii

Tomorrow,
we will raise
a tide towards you,
flush a swell against your form
and you so small to cope.

It is invasive to dive below
the sheltered surface
to unbaffle the explanation
of your body,

but there is a need
to mother you,
to distinguish your pulse
from hers.

There is a burning to count you
in toes and fingers,
map your limb lengths
and circumferences,

hear where the sounds
echo in your curves,
so that we can plot
where you will moor
when you arrive.

iii

You are brand new,
with days that when counted
don't take up
the fingers on one hand.

You are brand new,
with echoes of the one
who came before,

the one who filled those sleepsuits,
softening the fabric with her heat
so you don't have to.

Together we have been renewed.
A ballast in so small a form
should never be overlooked.

You are strength.
I can see it in the set of your neck,
the clench of limbs and features
as you stretch to take your place.

iv

Little cup of courage, you jump
off the round of the earth, unafraid
to spill yourself but you never lose a drop.
Your closed eyes trust the hammock of the dark.
It's enough to stop a heart.

You tug the rug of family to your chest,
all thought, your language sounds out
where we fall within these walls,
where our pictures rest. We cluster,
still, in your clenching fist.

Eager eggshell baby, your wolf-blue eyes
have shone since my scissors cut your cord.
Today, unwrap the earliest hour, the promises
uttered in the room where you breathed first.
Keep yourself for poetry, works of art.

Of my body you took nothing,
not cheek, nor chin, nor fingers, only
my vowels, warming syllables to fill your mouth,
but use me as a platform as you wish,
plant your feet, bend your knees, release.

I See My Bones In No Other

There is a place in the face of family
where all the other faces live.

There, bones and skin align to remind us
that we are merely segments of blistering fruit.

Without digging nails beneath familial skin,
there is a reflex to read everyone the same.

What else can happen when the set of an eyebrow can yield
where you come from, who you come from, who are your people.

But, baby girl, there is something more
than blood between us.

It is there in the way your small head sits between my jaw
and shoulder, in how your temple fits against my chin.

Maybe loving your mother changed me physically.
Maybe she opened my features so your blinking eyes can slow

against the side of my mouth, so your sleeping body
can shape into my waiting bones.

In Silhouette, The Change Is Clear

Your new height,
how you press against air,
claim more space in the room.

In black against sun, the change is clear;
your nose, chin, important structures —
shoulder and back stature.

In dust through light,
the falling particles matter, frame you
wash you in their air rushed marching.

In day against night, the change is clear;
these stretching moments are shaped
by the form you take.

We Settle Where Limbs Overlap

for Nova

Secure as artichoke leaves,
that neat weight and counterweight,
as your heart whirrs spoke-like
behind shoulder blade and rib.

Your back slopes warm along my arm.
Fingers bud in my shirt's stretched collar.
This evening owns only the tumble
of the washing machine, the lamp's low burn.

My senses learn the soft drag and push
of your breathing, the downy balm
of your baby hair, small magics begging me
to steal this moment somehow,

relish all of you while I can.
You will find a universe beyond
my arms vying for your notice
once you wake.

When Is The Rainbow, Momma?

We are at the point where conversations
take place in reflection,
your face and shoulders framed in the rear-view mirror.
You at nearly three seek disorder where there is none.

I expect anything but this, usual statements
of thirst or the urgency of an untied shoelace,
so with my mind on the distance to the house,
I placate with *"rainbows come after the rain,
                that's the rule."*

I glance into the glass, see synapse and sinew
connect what you know to what I tell you.

My answer is found wanting.

Who knew that words
would heap at the back of your mouth,
so you can slip them forward, dexterous
and articulate, as you need them.

Maybe these querying faculties steamed
into your vegetables
or soaped into your scalp
in your bath, or took a letter
from every time we questioned wildly
what green can be the colour of.

*"No momma, rainbows should come first,
        they're more important"*

And I cannot let it pass, though I should.
Can't leave you only light where there is dark,
so I tell you we need rain first to reward us with colour,
the softness of wet grass on dog paws,
the balm of the still puddle to the pebble.

I grip the wheel, feel the rain fall on us
in a way a three year old should never know.
As your mothers we stretch our brittle spines
to the limit of our material to keep you dry.

But I see in your eyes the moment you take off
at a run, tearing the fabric of fact to demand
only beauty, only truth.

A Record Of You

What can I keep of these first months
as you slip from my hands.

You are water I scoop with netted fingers,
words I hold in my mouth until my lips

are forced to open and I release you to the air.
You are information disseminated

and I have no control over your reception.
What do I choose of your facts, your necessities,

daily meals and sleeps,
the intangible cycle of our days together,

what to stack neatly
and what, if anything, to discard.

I want all of you to keep,
every breath, all your garbled syllables,

but in my cataloguing, I run the risk
of filing you too strictly,

losing you among labels,
rubber banded clusters of paper,

clothes you have outgrown,
socks that once held your tiny feet.

Seasons You Witness

Coast Road. April 2017

I consult my rear view,
learn that the gloss leaves
of your eyelids have breezed shut.

You are kept from the road's ripple
under car wheels,
sonic swell from the speakers.

As we wait together at the long lights,
I eye your soft recline,

a rapid meditation
on the seasons you witness
while you doze.

And I want to be present in your musings,
learning the stuff of your dreams.

But the green light shakes me,
my reflexes shift us forward,

past these whims
that are the nonsense wonders
of motherhood.

Spiddal, May 2017

Grass stains on her knees,
juice drops down her shirt,
she keeps tiny stones in polka dot pockets
to build small houses for her sister.

She twirls home smelling of suncream,
hair spun like blades of grass,
threads around threads,
eyes brighter than thought.
She's living the thrill
of being three in summertime
and she will gather this day
in her hands.

She hums in her chair,
talking her way through her snack,
crackers crumble as words race.
She's full of all that we can do –
You and me and Nova, Momma –
She conjures bog walks and donkeys,
whispers that she knows
which carrots are sweetest *for the baby*.

Her bag is packed for travel,
everything we need for our half-mile wander.
She leads us out the drive,
ears trained to hear
what's coming from a distance.
She plots a course past familiar ditches,
promises the flowers
she'll come back to collect them later.

Grass stains on her knees,
juice drops down her shirt,
she keeps tiny stones in polka dot pockets
to build small houses for her sister.

Ballyheigue, June 2017

My youngest love and I linger
between strand and playground.
Shrills of upward swings
and gusts skim in from Tralee Bay.
Wind whirls with January vigour
but she sleeps on, tucked in my arms
as June's breeze rocks us.

My eyes are on the scene by the sea,
seagulls taking turns
in the freefall of the breeze.
Below them, two of my loves
sweep out in line
with the waves' brushstrokes.
They move like they're trying to catch
all the colour before
it submerges in the sand.

I watch them shrink in curving trails
alongside waters
that have been travelling
since I was the girl filling
my small hands with shells.
It's a sprawling beach-walk day,
dogs swimming after sticks,
our coats are closed to the chin.
It's a day for warm coffee
in cold hands.

I wait for their return,
know they will come back to me.
This is as sure as the waters' churning,
as certain as sand and stone
are funnelling beneath
green-blue ripples
far out near the jutting rocks,
beyond my line of sight.

In A Minute

Wait a minute is a road built on floorboards,
      traffic jumbled in a chaos of pink plastic.
Give me a minute is an open door,
      her in coat and hat, fingers splayed on the doorframe.
In a minute is a zip clicking its way up her body,
      finding a home under her dimpled chin.

When time has no weight, how can a toddler keep
      the day in her hands.
For her there are no grains of sand, just
      "wait a minute, give me a minute, in a minute".
Her minutes are meals and colouring,
      sleeps and outside, always outside.

You can tell her everyone comes back in a minute,
      dinner will be cool in a minute.
But remember when there is no time,
      count the day her way,
in sandwiches and cut fruit,
      kisses and warm damp facecloths,
a sweaty forehead against your neck,
      soothed pains and belly tickles,
dancing and brushed teeth,
      stories about the rabbit and carrot soup.

Sweet things easily forgotten,
      when minutes pass without notice.

Myth In The Kitchen

for Juno

I'm peeling potatoes the first time you haul
your chair over ridges of uneven floor,
clamber to the summit of the kitchen sink.
You find me where I've been waiting for you, daughter.

We build rituals together, you and I,
observe ceremonies in this March brightness as simple
as the passing of potatoes from your small hands to mine.
And I have you, spud after spud, until your attention creeps

along the countertop, coming to land on the loose pyramid
of fruit bruising the scales. All lit up, you list the tastes
you prefer, *pears apples bananas* till your tongue stumbles
on the blushing stranger. As your mouth strains to name it,

I teatowel my blade, section the swell
so you can smell the juice bursting. Uneasy
at how I pull and bend the skin, pluck seeds
deft as feathers, you think my theft too rough, so I offer

you a jewel glinting between my thumb and fingertip.
You weigh my tribute and I reread all the poems
about the first girl to suffer from myth.
Were her eyes as blue with trust as yours?

I've learned literature's warnings, but somehow you know gift
from guillotine. I brace for the transfer, my hand to yours,
slow and sure, and you rewrite the ending,
use my frame to withstand the burden of legacy.

You watch the vessel burst, revel in the pink of destruction.
It's in this bloom of colour that the world opens for you.
Your future stirs when you climb from your perch,
myths recast as you strand me in your wake.

But I will stay here and wait for you, daughter.
My mothering hands will cradle the chaos you discard.

The Trees And The Breeze

When she turns her face towards you,
the half-moon of her silhouette backlit by late October,
she asks *"what is god, Mammy?"*

Quick as a tongue against teeth
with words that sound like they are all thought
you crouch, turn her to the view,

the red lemonade leaves of the Cherry Blossom,
dripping silver of the Birch peeking through moss.
You tell her to look and with eyes so like yours, she looks.

You say *"my god is the trees and the breeze."*
At two, she knows both tangibles, has understood
your idea of god against the soft peach of her cheek,

her baby chin, her tongue in the rain falling,
wind on that sliver of skin where her wool hat fails to kiss her eyebrows,
how air teases fingers poking from pink sleeves, too busy to keep
    their gloves.

She counts and stores in her mind all the parts of your god that are hers,
the mess of Cherry Blossoms by the gate,
her big curving Birch with the fairy door healed into the bark.

She has walked the tiny stone path of the fairies to that tree's base,
laid her palm flat on the trunk to read the story of the knots.
She tells us how butterflies visit its mossy coat for their dinner,

knows that trusting the tree with the press of her hands will steady her,
that she can stretch up from her feet, let her spine and head tilt back
and between the strength of Birch and the dark Spiddal soil,

she is safe to raise her face and peer up through the offset
    rungs of branches,
to see her world mapped in clouds that linger in the cold
    Connemara sky.

These Nights

We meet in the dead hum,
at what used to be Ryanair flight time,
when on a fiver we'd drop it all and go,
hole up in a one-star hotel room
and know only the heat
of each other for a week.

These nights we pass in the hallway,
bare feet light against tiles.
Your mission: warm water to soothe.
Mine: milk to lure a dreamer back to sleep.
Our love is awake in this house,
corners filled with family
we didn't account for on any boarding card.

And at this knee-sore hour
with your shoulders drooped
in tired falling, part of me is waiting
at the door for you,
straining to hear you shuffle
across the floor,

a single bag tight in your hands,
as we leave this all behind
to explore all we have yet to see.

From You I Want

I want to know this little is enough —
the rolling cadence of our kitchen rituals,
all talk cut short, warm drinks abandoned

to steep thickly on countertops
while we whirl always to the next room,
answer some sweet shrill or other.

I want you to tell me that as little
as black coffee in the car by the bay
is enough to keep each other.

We cost nothing but the time
we no longer have to give.
Now we are undrunk glasses of wine

swirling down the sink at midnight.
We are 4am feeds and bowls of cereal
in the flaring dark.

But I remember you before real life
mattered, all fire and softness,
and I just need to know in my bones

that you're with me still, even in this hallway
as we shrug them into coats,
pull hats down around their ears,

preparing them to step out
into their day.

For She Who Loves Me

She's scribbling promises again,
making plans where she knows I'll find them.

Today, she collects treefall with our girls,
all neighbour-windowsill chatter, her easy closed-gate lean.

She presses leaves to brown paper, shows our eldest
that colour means each season can be savoured,

how not everything is lost
because Momma cried on the drive home.

I watch from my corner as she leads small hands
towards questions in the Connemara wall.

It's as if this Autumn garden understands
how treasure translates to tiny fingers.

And when the three come in, soil-soft hands hiding
in wells of coat sleeves, her promises are held there too,

in small palms and the way they hold my face,
how I feel necessary under their touch –

how in the evening when I'm grief low,
she lends me her weight, definite as a vow

because she knows how pain can unmoor a body.
She has seen enough in the turning of tides to promise

that what arrives will ebb again. She reminds me
that nothing roots us more than gravity.

Epilogue

Say

Say we unknit our limbs,
pull apart where veins bramble,
return to those early days,
raze all that we have built.

Say we never curled beside shadowed columns,
never slipped thumbs in old bullet wounds
while we waited for each other to alight
from odd numbered buses.

Say in searching for you in the lights
of the top deck, instead I lost you
to a different stop, watched someone else
step to meet you and walk you into their evening.

What a life we would have squandered
by losing each other in that loose time,
when Spring winds chilled those Dublin bridges,
plumed Liffey spray to mist
across the boundaries of your body.

The Road, Slowly

We idle in the fall between foot plants,
rise with the ditches, down again with the drains.

On this Tuesday, buggy wheels trundle in the lulls
of staring cattle and January fields.

The neighbours all claim your notice
and I'm so glad we're raising you with manners.

The whole road yours, grass tufts and gravel,
the Rottweiler rattling his stable yard chain.

At your height, the world is all wall and bracken,
stone and puddle, you don't know the horizon.

But as your sister babbles, your eyes shift
to the birds, lake and sea in the one view,

water that isn't always storybook blue,
but shades of the weather, as we are.

Notes

WOMEN POETS TEACH ME HOW TO BE A WOMAN:

The phrases "The Yellow Room", "the rabbit's foot" and "all night I felt their absence and I burned" refer to the poem "Warming Her Pearls" by Carol Ann Duffy (*Selling Manhattan*, Anvil Press Poetry, 1987).

The phrase "love with an almost fearful love" refers to Sharon Olds' poem "Bathing the Newborn" (*Selected Poems*, Jonathan Cape, 2005).

The phrase "hoisting to an attic's dark" comes from the poem "Mining" by Rebecca Goss (*Her Birth*, Carcanet, 2013).

The phrase "the art of losing isn't hard to master" comes from the poem "One Art" by Elizabeth Bishop (*The Complete Poems 1926-1979*, Farrar, Straus & Giroux, 1979).

Originally from Tralee, Co Kerry, LIZ QUIRKE lives in Spiddal, Co. Galway with her wife and daughters. Quirke's poetry has appeared in many publications, including *New Irish Writing* in *The Irish Times*, *Irish Examiner*, *Southword*, *Crannóg*, *The Stony Thursday Book*, *One* (Jacar Press, US), *The Ofi Press* (Mexico) and Eyewear Publishing's *The Best New British and Irish Poets 2016*. She was the winner of the 2017 Listowel Writers' Week Originals Short Poem Competition, the 2016 Dromineer Literary Festival Flash Fiction Competition, the 2015 Poems for Patience competition and the 2012 Doneraile Literary Festival Edmund Spenser Poetry Prize. She was shortlisted for the Cúirt New Writing Prize in 2015 and nominated for a Hennessy Literary Award in 2016. She holds degrees from University College Cork, Dublin City University and NUI Galway. She is a PhD researcher at NUI Galway.

www.lizquirke.com

www.salmonpoetry.com

"Like the sea-run Steelhead salmon that thrashes upstream to its spawning ground, then instead of dying, returns to the sea – Salmon Poetry Press brings precious cargo to both Ireland and America in the poetry it publishes, then carries that select work to its readership against incalculable odds."

TESS GALLAGHER